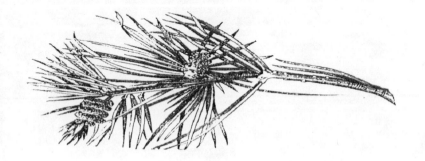

Winter Vision

Winter Vision

Robert M. Giannetti

Cashes Valley Publishing

2011

ISBN: 978-0-9740680-2-2

Library of Congress Control Number: 2011908721

Manufactured in the United States of America

First Edition

16 15 14 13 12 11   1 2 3 4 5 6 7 8 9 10

Book design by Pamela Kohn, Professional by design
www.ProfByDesign.com

Cover illustration by Joan Turrell

Cashes Valley Publishing
P.O. Box 2714, Niagara Falls, NY 14302
CashesValleyPubl@roadrunner.com

Dedication

This book is dedicated to the memory of my uncle, Michael Orange, who passed away in 2010. In my early childhood, after his return from service with the U.S. Navy in World War II, he was instrumental in stimulating my enduring interest in literature and classical music. Although he did not have an extensive formal education, he read widely and was a learned man. His regard for my poetry in his later years was comforting and sustaining. I miss him.

Acknowledgments

Several of the poems in this book previously appeared in *Slipstream, Mythic Passages, Lewiston-Porter Sentinel,* and *Temat* (a Polish periodical of arts and letters).

Joan Turrell graciously permitted a leaf from her exquisite artist's book, *Winter Vision,* to be used for the cover of the book you now hold in your hands. Joan's work is a visual rendering of lines from my poem of the same name.

In 2009, Dariusz Lebioda, distinguished scholar and poet from Bydgoscz, Poland, translated a number of my poems into Polish and published them, along with a lengthy critical essay on my work, in *Temat.*

Following the publication of my work in *Temat,* I was honored with an invitation to the 32nd November of Poetry, an international festival held in Poznan, Poland in 2009, where I gave readings in academic and community settings with honorees from other countries spanning Europe, Asia, and Africa. Several months later in 2010, *Slipstream* sponsored my reading at the Poetry Collection of the University at Buffalo, where I first presented many of the new works printed here.

Robert Borgatti, an editor of *Slipstream*, made a video of the program for the Poetry Collection's archives, and its Curator, Michael Basinski, mounted a special exhibit of items related both to my poetry and to my interest in fine and rare books, displaying some gems from the world famous collection.

These events were covered extensively in the press and I am most appreciative of the articles written by Michele DeLuca of the *Niagara Gazette*, Teresa Sharp of the *Buffalo News*, and Terry Duffy of the *Lewiston-Porter Sentinel*.

I have been fortunate to count a much admired poet of international distinction and a fellow Lewistonian, Danuta Kostewicz, as a friend and colleague. Her strong and continuing interest in my work and her sound counsel have meant much to me.

Lee Passarella has also been an interested reader of my work for a number of years and I am grateful for his friendship.

On a personal note I would be remiss not to mention my fine family, and indeed my wife Rita's entire extended family in Western New York, who have shown the flag at literary events where I have read my poetry.

Contents

1

Commitment

Winter Vision

In the Natural Light

Natural History Museum

A Theme is Not a Melody

Robert M. Giannetti

COMMITMENT

I resist as best I can
the forgetting of my dream
drifting into and out of dozes, cat naps,
awakening and writing in the dark,
trying not to fall back asleep
with glittering day ahead —
the dawn coming
for me in a world for my making.
I resolve to get up go as far as I can
before another drift
into another sleep.

I once made poetic gestures,
my callow youth blurring the lines
of poetry, drama and utter prose.
I now gesture again
in the fullness of imagination
recording once unrecorded
and discarded dreams
seeing and remembering
in starts from the sudden dark
what has continued beyond
my wildest wonder.

The line is no longer blurred,
as I bring this dream to you, my reader,
glowing in my knowing

that it has been worth
the emerging
from the long sleep that awakens into life.
And as the drowsy time comes on again
I will not fail to keep and set down
every dream I can, for you.

WINTER VISION

Winter trees,
their leafless branches brittle as thinning hair,
open the view from the path,
exposing the bare hills beyond,
now visible in the distance.

Summer's cover of billowing,
dense green lushness
has given way
to grey, bony shapes,
the chisel of biting air,
the sculpture of the cold.
The scant light parceled out
in the shortened day
makes precious the blush of color
on the rosy cheeks of a sunrise
beckoning across the vacant landscape,
arousing my ardor, leaving a lust
to continue the journey
through whatever
remains of the day.

IN THE NATURAL LIGHT

In the natural light of the early morning
I look out at the laurels:
twenty-five degrees by the porch thermometer.
I can always tell it's that temperature
by looking at those tight bunches of green
stitched among the spreading pines.
The fronds huddle together
for warmth,
like freezing birds
hunched down upon themselves.
By squeezing so close together in the cold,
they leave more space around them
for the eye to take in the background
of browns, the fallen leaves, the trunks,
the bark of standing trees —
the change in temperature
gifting a changing rhythm
of shades and colors coming and going
along the mountain creek in winter.

Down on the banks of the creek
my gaze settles upon
the old rotted tree
amid the boulders
in the cold, bright froth
at the water's edge.
One finger's pressure

would probably topple it over,
its inside hollowed out,
its crumbling, moldy bark
a bare shell to the sight.

It was standing there
when my uncles visited long ago
and a little bird came repeatedly
to perch on one of those bare,
stick-like branches
that still stretches over the creek.
I don't want to see that tree go,
but I am sure a new rhythm
will be brought to the scene when it does,
and the toppling over will open up
new possibilities to the eye.

What a way for the world to run.
But that is how it is.
Whatever more there is
will be what comes
in the place of that tree.

The tree itself will disintegrate
beyond recognition
into the earth,
and some remnants

of its dusty remains
taken into the wind.

Life is a breathing of death.
The pulmonary movements
of the changing air, pulsing
rhythms great and small,
carry random particles,
waves of energy,
like inchoate memories,
forever and ever
to scenes anew.

NATURAL HISTORY MUSEUM

My granddaughter refused
to go back
into the natural history museum —
into the noise
and into the crush
of the crowd, suddenly
unable to bear
the sight of the dead,
the stuffed animals,
the plaster casts of the extinct,
or hear any more
of the planetarium show,
the babble about
the stars, the sun,
the very earth –
all to be lost
and in time confined
to an unspeakable end.

We went outside
and sat quietly for a time
beside one another
in the open air —
the rush of our years
slowed
to a stillness
and a serene silence.

A THEME IS NOT A MELODY

I could never explain to him that
a theme is not a melody —
that the tuneful phrase
was not supposed to go on and on, only
a few notes here and there,
what he called "the good parts" getting lost,
driven at times under ground
suddenly surfacing at unexpected turns
as the "deep" composition moved
through mysterious passages.

Had he lived long enough
I could have explained it
to him in terms of what
I now remember about
my childhood
and my time with him.

It was never a simple melody in my mind.
And it didn't go on and on —
a few notes remembered
here and there long after his death —
the good parts for a while lost
in a counterpoint of past and present,
their subtle strains somehow recapitulated
in good time and creating a symphonic composition,
its structure perceived only now in retrospect,

but still unresolved,
the key to its understanding modulating
note by note into the mystery
of what has yet to be played
and needs to be listened to.

2

Wildflowers

Afternoon Sun

The Studio of Life

Landscape

Pears

WILDFLOWERS

Age has brought me to this road
of wildflowers,
a road I drive in my own time
no longer in panic
about starting out again
to make my way,
driven by necessity or by pride,
thinking only of another destination,
another purpose.

On this late summer's drive
I come to revel in the rousing persistence
of the wildflowers along the highway –
Queen Anne's lace stretching
from North to South
down vast strands of roadway,
joined by running riots
of Joe Pye and Black-Eyed Susan,
their yellows and lavenders popping up
up through the delicate white cover.
A tireless conversation of light and shadow
takes the measure of it all,
urging me on and on,
mile after mile, and I am
heedless of where or when
I may have to exit,
or what I might find there.

AFTERNOON SUN

In the glow I am unable

to recall when I first came

through these deep shadows

to the light pouring through the leaves,

and as I lean into an easy and familiar feeling

of belonging to all the sun casts itself upon

and sculpts into illumination,

I accept

in the numinous embrace

the warm and searing mystery

of holding and of losing all.

THE STUDIO OF LIFE
... FOR DANUTA

Hope comes in the door in photographs
                                delivered
by chance on a clouded day,
                a studio of life
in a clear plastic envelope
beckoning remembrance of a black and white world —
post-War Europe in the early Sixties –
formative years for the solitary soul
as for the world — notes
echoed from a distance,
tuning the mind
to the scale of being
as it was and still is
in the images flowing
across time and the table
they are spread upon.

There is a glow coming from the eyes
of the nameless faces in the photographs.
In the era of their excitement, their hope
reaches out to capture the gaze
of current spectators — just beyond
the reach of their life on this earth, poised
on the edge of eternal regard.

LANDSCAPE

Ground and sky swell in a chorus
                    of the coming storm —
at the painting's lower edge are soft sounds of sopranos
                    in the swaying green grass
momentarily catching the shifting light before
dusky altos enter and drift toward a darkening center,
there blending into dense harmonies
with baritones and bassos on the bold brown earth.
Above, piercing tenors from an icy black sky
unfold rhythmic strands of sharp silver clouds echoing
shadowed shapes on the ground below.

No music of the spheres here
and no need for any other distant hope or expectation,
even of a more sunny day to paint or compose.
The senses find their destiny, their ecstasy,
in praise of what is,
in life as in art — numinous —
in any weather,
wholly holy,
now and forever —
                    Amen.

PEARS

Pears are autumn's emblem,

green shading to brown,

juice laden like the moist

softening ground, ripening

in the burdened boughs

swaying in the slanting sun,

then bountifully dropping all around.

We take and eat

of this body,

given up for us

by the earthen god

we know now

and forever. Amen.

3

STILL LIFE

Nothing, nothing
is more perfect
than the light that shines
in this instant through the window
on the simple wooden basket
heaped with rocks
randomly set beside
an old rush broom
in the corner of the cabin,
deep shadows
brushing over the golden
spruce paneled wall behind.
It is the power and the glory
of the light that bestows
a simple and profound wonder
upon the rapt and silent man,
upon his silent dog,
once and forever seeing
life everlasting, amen.

ENNOBLEMENT

The approach of winter
is demanding attention.

The sky, losing the lingering color
 taken from sparse leaves hanging

on trees soon to be bare,
will leave only an inner song

to relieve the cold
and starkness of the snow —

when flake upon flake will be pressed
to the earth with heavy steps

and labored breaths will condense
into the old familiar air

of fine and fleeting wisps intoning
the enduring pride of life.

MORNING WALK

Leaving committee rooms
                    and their lives behind,
I have seen men get up
in illness or exhaustion
unmindful and vacant of awareness,
as they slipped away
                    from noise and commotion,
turning their backs and walking out
                                    to sink
into the darkness,
the silent stillness
of winter graveyards.

Many a morning
multitudes of stone markers
emerge in the dawn to greet me,
solitary as I walk my dog,
bounding with excitement
                    through the deep snow.

We sense the sun rising
                    and keep moving
Through the lifting darkness
And the cold open air
                    above the covered earth.

LIPS

In the dusk of a pale grey day
on a winter walk in the park
I came upon the trunks
of several small trees stretching
across the top of a chain link fence
around a ball field.
Where they touched the fence,
their bark seemed like lava
that had once flowed
over the rail and was now
hardened in distended flaps,
lip-like, pursed tightly
over the cold metal.

Summer's shade had hidden
those lips, veiling their grip
as the tree tops swayed to find
some opening to the light.
How easily missed on a stroll,
were it not now
for the leafless winter branches,
the bare spaces
exposing those lips
in their determined
kiss.

ONLOOKERS

Barely rising above
the tall bright prairie grass
in which they stand —
in a lost time,
a place in the Old West —
a woman and a babe in arms
appear in the open land,
their image now present
in a fading and brittle print
drawing slow silent breaths
from onlookers.

In that swaying grass
the woman and the babe once
heard the click of a shutter
locking them there,
stilling the wind and holding
the shadows they
peer beyond.

4

ENCOUNTER AT THE GORGE

Osprey in the air
                    reaching
Dog's feet on the ground
                            treading

Man's feet shoed —
                separated from the earth
Reach limited
          by arm's length
Only imagination
                    capable
Of feeling the earth
                as a dog might
Or rising into the sky
                    as a bird might

At the top of the deep gorge
above the river
the osprey lifts into view,
suddenly at eye level
with the man walking his dog
at the rim. Bird and man
stare silently
into one another's eyes.
The dog barks and braces,
lifting his gaze and
rearing up on hind legs,

insistent excitement sounding for all
the sudden, unfathomable wonder
of shared and solitary being.

ROADSIDE AMERICA

You missed it — go back
at the next exit.

Go back to a world created
in the first half of the 20th Century,
a world long a thought
in the mind of its maker,
taking form over many years
of labor in some obscure workshop —
a basement or a garage,
the vision springing from
a model railroad display
enlivened with a multitude
of other little structures, buildings
and scenes along the tracks.

Once set in motion, hard
to stop, to be content, to rest.
With one thing leading to another,
the design expanded.
A space on the side of the tracks
between the grove of trees and
the waterfall descending
into the valley —
an ideal location for a gas station
on the roadway coming out of town.
An empty stretch on the mountain above —

ideal for an incline railroad.
And then the maker, put in mind
of his idyllic village back
in the Old Country,
somehow made a place for it,
backfilling, fitting it in,
historical remembrance casting
the scene a little out of scale
with the rest,
as had happened
in other places
along the different gauges of running track.

We now gaze upon
a lost but enduring world
honored in its display,
illuminated by lamps
from above, but mainly from within
the multitude
of little buildings, all emitting
a glow that shines through the windows
from little hidden bulbs inside.

We marvel at the day
passing into night and back again
inside the exhibit hall —
glimpsing in the darkness a

a world yet to see interstate highways,
a world asleep without the hum of traffic,
a world whose brightest lights glowed
in the heart of the city, at the roadside factory,
its night shift faithful in industry
to the break of day.

As the lights in the hall
come on again from above,
the sunrise reveals a multitude
of trees in their faded autumn colors,
old fabrics from the maker's loom
seeking to give bright contrast
to the dusty green carpet of grass.

We come to all this
and marvel as before
a shrine —
entranced road-weary pilgrims,
captivated and contemplative,
hearkening to a revelation
made known off the Interstate.

You missed it — go back
at the next exit.

ORIENT POINT

The salt wind is intense
coming off the whitecaps
and the air turns cool
in the hanging call and stir of autumn.
Grains of blowing sand scour
everything
under the low grey expanse
of clouded sky.
Water laps up
in froth around
the deserted beach.

No need here to pose anything,
to try to capture
the objects scattered all around.
Driftwood, grass, stones, sand —
all composed and re-composed,
continuously brushed and cropped,
heedless of camera lens or
artist's ordering eye.

All around is the relentless breeze,
breathed in at first
with a conscious gulp,
held for a moment
in the round of the ribs,
and then exhaled

into passing time,
savored at the scant margin,
the edge
of the life-giving, all-forgetting
sea.

CITY HUNGER

I felt the air move across my face
and heard the sound of flapping wings
as I got out of the car in the driveway.
I saw it was not just one set of wings,
but maybe a dozen or more.
I stood in place
stock still in wonder.
A flock of cedar waxwings
was devouring the berries
on the potted holly tree
alongside the front steps.
So abandoned in their feeding,
they flurried but did not flee
at my presence — exposing
the bright band at the end
of their tails as they busied
their beaks with the berries.

I broke away at last
to go into the house,
and half the flock took off
in flight as I climbed the steps.
The other half hardly
looked up from their feeding.
And soon
those that had bolted
began to return,

all busy back on the tree
by the time I opened my door.

The bird books call them
gregarious, feeding in flocks
on berries in open spaces.
They mention nothing
of their appearance
in densely populated urban areas
with hardly another
standing cache of berries
to be seen.
Somehow they had found
the potted holly tree
in all the brick and cement
around the town home.
They took the gift of the berries
as I in turn took the gift
of their presence.
In that continuing commotion
of air and sound, the birds
soon left that potted tree
bare of its berries.
Under the sweep
of the vast and limitless sky,
the consuming rapture had come
and gone.

FOR NO REASON AT ALL

For no reason at all the happiness

has come upon me again.

It's not yet even fall,

but a rustle of color is in my heart

and everything sounds like a New Age piano,

an accompaniment to a tune yet unsung,

unending runs, chords

as bright as the underside of leaves

that turn in the wind,

taking silver from the night

and giving it to the day.

It is enough:

all that can be, and will ever be

in a world whose eternity

is of my own making,

a moment fixed

in splendor,

finding and holding

what need not be reached for.

5

The Hunt

Riff

Insight

The Harrowing

Golgotha in Tennessee

THE HUNT

In the caves at Lascaux
they tried to describe what
they saw, their scratching
the rough rigors of praise —

praise of the world,
the life
of the majestic, powerful animals
they penned in the room
of their imagination,
keeping vivid
in the scant light
of smoky fires,
the stunning wonder
of what had been hunted down
and set on the wall.

RIFF

The jazzman plays off
the beaten path.
No simple whistler he.

He looks at his tune in the mirror —
head-on – in profile –
wide-eyed – squinting —
in the darkness of closed lids
the sound of light
suddenly coming into his eyes.

Holding the key
to remembrance,
he modulates
to forgetfulness, and back again,
his harmonic turns and echoes
in tempo rubato taking
his syncopated soliloquy
where it will.

Channeling grace notes
providentially dropped
into
the passing moment — he cradles endless
flowers from a crannied wall.
They unfold in glissando
and sail

in rapture
across the big, wide, wonderful
ocean
of sound.

INSIGHT

Ultimate meaninglessness stared me
in the face.
Why should it be depressing?
The way of the world will always be
what it will,
changing to suit the observer,
himself unobserved in his departure.
It is all a matter of time,
which is ultimately unkept.
So it is that we come down to
what is now
before us,
and in the mirror of consciousness
we know we cannot grasp
what we see.

Without a mirror
the eyes cannot see themselves.
We wandered around for millennia
as a race, only seeing ourselves
in occasional puddles
left by the rain,
or when standing at the edge
of a pond, or the sea,
ready to fall
in love with the vision, impetuously
risking the plunge to possess it,

or sadly turning away and going again
down the aimless trails that criss-cross
the lands of the earth —

trampling the bones of former wanderers,
the remains of countless animals,
the dwellings turned to dust,
the middens of discarded matter
heaping the ground higher and higher,
rolling up in the dense darkness
a tighter and tighter ball,
all that went before spinning
in a void with no mirror,
or one that the onlooker has turned away from,
as I turn away from
the scribblings on this page
with nothing more to be said.

THE HARROWING

The log-sided chimney frame came down today.
It looked sound to the glancing eye
but its insides were rotten to the touch —
a weathered, stately totem at the side of the cabin,
drenched in summer's rains, and dried
brittle in the fall winds and many a winter's stare.

The carpenter delivered the quietus,
tearing off some black, shaded pieces
and revealing the hidden sepulcher within —
the accumulated moisture,
wet particle board and crumbling studding,
pieces of log siding surrendering
to the rough surgery
of his hands.

The chimney was soon down,
its broken remains irreverently tossed
on the ground among the decaying leaves,
their once remarkable autumn colors
dulled and diminished, occasionally lifted
by the chilling wind
across the bare, unobstructed space
where the structure had long endured.
As the dusk turned into night,

it gave little promise of what
the carpenter said he would raise anew
in that dark, empty space
at the break of dawn.

GOLGOTHA IN TENNESSEE

Three giant wooden crosses
towering over a highway
on a hill in Tennessee —
        shocked and stunned
        would the faithful be
        in their rolling Southern
        syllables to see
        those crosses in my eyes,
        counting it a strabismus
        of belief not to see
        this road a route to a harvest
        for Jesus,
        and all those passing by
        inclined
        to satisfy the hungry lord.
All I see atop
this gruesome hill
is what is left
after the money changers
have raided the temple,
salesmen — in church as in state
and in the Decalogue of business —
hawking unseen salvation,
telling it from the mountain
and down the decline
of devilish addiction
to be repented in leisure,

saving the soul that
still clutches its ill-gotten gains.
        Saved simply by saying so
        say the three crosses
        in the Tennessee wilderness,
        on a promontory
        from which the Christ
        and the two thieves beside him
        have jumped —
        from the greed and the glory
        to the rough places below
        on the valley floor,
        angels failing to waft them,
        powerless to banish
        the greed, the corruption,
        the prissy and hollow Puritanism,
        the wars, the lies and the deceit
        dragging the Christ and the thieves
        in their all too human bodies down
        to the jagged rock of ages below.
No one is hanging
on those crosses it is clear
on that hill in Tennessee.
I speed past them,
their tawdry and intrusive statement
leaving it difficult to imagine

a god's in a heaven
and all might be made
right with the world.

6

Tempests

Passing Away

Nature's God

Hummingbirds

Snow

TEMPESTS

A chamber group is playing a piece called *The Tempest,*
its music summoning up Shakespeare's farewell
                               to the theatre,
a late romance, a tragedy fully matured
                             into an enduring comedy.
A veritable Miranda is in the audience a few seats away.
Looking at her I can readily take up the part of a
                             Caliban,
imagining myself nudging away the young Ferdinand
at her side, placing the threadbare cloak of my lust over her,
feeling her nipples harden, her hips move in rhythms
                             roused
by the musical murmurs, the dramatic visions of wonder,
the rapt excitement of a brave new world.
In the pretty, prancing gambol of her youth
she gives no heed to the homely hunger that besets my age.
Languidly she holds the safe, soft hand of her Ferdinand,
as mystified as he by the ethereal sway of youthful fantasy,
fantasy that will show itself sadly corporeal, after all,
in time's unimagined decline, its consuming fire,
its unquenched thirst.

I can no longer play the part of a guileless Ferdinand.
But the grotesque, libidinous desperation of a Caliban?
That, the only figure to be cut by an old man
who looks with interest at a young girl?
That, or the fatherly cast of a Prospero, the old magician,

hearing the humming sounds in her nubility,
and composing a protective world about her,
while sexless Ariel, blithe spirit, hovering over this
wrenching drama,
rises with unseen sound from the loamy earth,
seeking only to be set free
before that magician renounces all his art in the end —
the play, the great globe itself, all finished and done.

The recital is over and Miranda now cleaves
like Eve to the side of her Ferdinand as she trails
out of the hall, innocently naked in spirit,
leaving that old play, this musical evocation of it,
and my bemused, persistent lust behind.
She will now be taking up life's part —
                              marriage, children, maturity,
and time will play upon that fine body
that I would readily kiss and caress, blessing
her slender youth before she knows, and rues,
what her flesh will too soon become.

The lingering harmonics of the music I have heard
haunt me in their passing,
as do the characters of the old valedictory drama
that found a flicker of life briefly again in this recital hall,

now an empty hollow place in which I no longer see
the sweet Miranda and can only nod
                              to melancholy modulations
of morbid thought in vanishing time —
the magic that held fast,
and nestled that young woman
in my unknown and unheeded gaze,
all too quickly fading
into the insubstantial air,
a storm gone,
leaving not a rack behind.

PASSING AWAY

The kind of perfume you'd smell
in a funeral parlor
trailed off a woman trudging
aimlessly into the store
lugging a shopping bag —
the vapor of her appearance
lingering in her departure —

not the bright face of
a beaming woman,
proud, emitting a glow
delighting the eyes,
stirring the strong fantasy that
she is capable of coupling with
at any time, anywhere,
because she is young,
and supple, and coiffed,
with boots that cover the calf
and leave a space between knee
and thigh inviting
a long lingering glance —

rather only a passing vision
of slow and sad decline
that offers a spritz of bad perfume
to capture attention.

NATURE'S GOD

Can you imagine the hunger of an animal,
waking up in the morning, starving, ready
to kill something
to ease the pain —
something smaller,
old, feeble,
or young, vulnerable?
Culling, killing —
surviving —
as does the hungry god
of human imagination —
killing to survive —
one order of lower life
yielding to another's
claws and teeth —
here — and gone.

HUMMINGBIRDS

A pair of hummingbirds swept up
to the newly stained walls,
the cabin resplendent before them
like a temple.
They hovered in awe.
Was it the color, or the fumes,
or a deeper, more arcane
allure, so fresh on the walls?

Butternut they call the stain,
but what did the hummingbirds
know that day?
They flew right up and
beat their wings
thousands of times
in ecstasy,
savoring the sweet smell,
the sticky stain drawing
their beaks forward,
little bodies shimmering
under the haze of their wings.

At first adoring, enraptured
by the seeming transubstantiation,

they knew better in the end.
Their beaks might have stuck to the walls
had they touched
the heavenly stain.
Upon consideration
they suddenly turned
and were gone.

SNOW

The snow this day is endless, enveloping
and persistent,
covering the land —
a silent, stately background
against which senseless calculation
brazenly belittles the serenity of contemplation.
The time and patience to dwell upon
the shapes and sizes,
the density of the flakes,
as they slowly fall in the natural light —
all lost
to the glaring rituals of speed —
squandering time —
all the many Inuit words for the snow
unimaginable and unnecessary.
Black print on white paper
surrenders to screen-lit flashes
with no foreground or background,
nothing tangible filling the unreal space.
Cold shoulders of sensibility somewhere shrug.
There is nowhere to tread
and there are no footprints in the snow.

7

Chapel in the Woods
Loss
White Butterfly
The Bundle
Mice

CHAPEL IN THE WOODS

Unexpectedly
the path through the forest opens
to reveal
warm shadows on the walls
of the nearby wooden structure —
so unlike the cold stone
and spiked spires
of cathedrals and basilicas.

In the turn of the seasons
from softly surging spring
through summer's press
and fall's slow surrender
to the waiting winter light,
the low belfry responds
to the attention of the standing trees,
setting them at ease in their vigilance.
The chapel's portals invite entry
into an embrace
of shelter shaped from the living earth,
beckoning rest on the wooden benches,
so unlike the cold slabs
on which lifeless effigies
lie and stare mercilessly
from atop the tombs
in gothic caverns,
heedless of the seasons
and their glory.

LOSS

I wanted to call and talk with him today
because it was snowing,
and I wanted to tell him,
so far away, how it came down
and how it lay
its white drapery over
the main street — all as in
a child's glass bubble, with floating specks
like coruscating stars
glinting in the grey daytime sky —
but he is gone
and cannot be reached
in the silence
that grips the words
and gasps in wonder.

WHITE BUTTERFLY

It has rained hard twice today
and each time a white butterfly
has passed across the windows
of the cabin afterwards.

No need to spin
a suggestion
of Noah releasing the dove,
or even the great Paraclete hovering
over the rushing waters
of the creek below.

For me, these white wings
have carried away the folly
of the want of anything else:
for the coming of the sun,
for the clearing of things unclear,
for the need of more than
what is here, unknown,
in the stillness of my mind,
sublime.

THE BUNDLE

I wanted to unwrap the little body
swaddled in the blankets
as it withered away,
perhaps by seeing it,
in whatever state it was,
to feel again
the exultation of happy discovery
and rapt engagement —

defying fatigue and decline,
embracing the mystery of joy,
pondering and propounding
the rhythms of creation,
the uniqueness, the individuation,
the emergence from the nameless,
surrounding void —

not
this decline, this wasting,
this sudden, gripping chill
that awakens me this morning
and sends me in utter confusion
and fright to this scrap of paper,
the fate of the swaddled body
in the bundle of blankets
unknown.

MICE

I am still primal, territorial,
I realized, as a mouse
suddenly appeared before me
on the cabin floor, popping up
as I worked on the computer,
taunting me to chase him down,
search after and destroy him,
prompting me to stake out my domain,
the inviolability of my space —

space I would not have cared
was mine, sitting at my desk, until
my double-take
at the mouse on the floor,
as if it were a double-click
with my metaphorical mouse,
opened up a window into
virtual awareness — a vision
of the sands and the valleys,
the firesides I huddled around
with other hominids,
and the stream beds
I dragged myself across, pointing
to the twisted roots of the tree
in drought exposed on the far bank —

questing after knowledge
and trapped
in the terrifying and determined
program of existence.

8

Darkness and Light

How's the Weather?

Closing My Journal Entry

Nostalgia

Creation

DARKNESS AND LIGHT

Stuck between the urge to flee
and the pull
back into the well of the past —
brought on by hearing songs
of thirty years ago,
I desire still another youthful act
of blind courage to propel me
into a future I've just now
come to know.
What's behind keeps welling
up, again, as if
I didn't know where it led.
Full-sighted blindness
I once had, and now
struggle with the light that haunts
my near-sighted eyes.
Once upon a time I peered
through the dark, and wondered
about what now has come upon me
in dazzling light.
I have nowhere else to go.

HOW'S THE WEATHER?

A gripping struggle for stability
plays out for hours in the sky:
clouds cast in plate tectonics, slabs
of grey and white under blue,
slide across the sun —
relentless aftershocks
of an early morning snow.
It came on at dawn here
in the mountains
in the collision of night
and day demanding
a last stand of winter before
inevitable surrender to the bright beauty
of bursting spring.

My father always used to ask
about the weather
in the all too few
telephone calls I had with him
after leaving home.
It must have been hard for him,
rooted as he was,
to keep up with me,
moving over so many climes
of the country, as incomprehensible
to him as my befuddlement

over his repeated inquiries
about the weather.
Did he then sometimes listen
for the exchange
of inner and outer dialogue
that I now hear so strongly,
or was he just making conversation,
after all?
Why did we never have
a long talk about the turn
of the seasons, or the roll
of the day?
A quarter century after his death
it is as hard to bring the matter
into still and steady focus
as it is for the mind's eye
or the painter's hand
to stop the unending dance
of light and of shadow.
Changes in the weather bring
his question to mind from time to time,
and I keep trying to answer it
better than I once did.

CLOSING MY JOURNAL

                for tonight,
leaving these fossilized
traces, these footprints
leading to a place
I do not know —
footprints that may never
again be seen
once I have passed,
or one day discovered
in sedimentary rock,
possibly fragmented,
tantalizing pieces
of what went before
and continued after,
assembled into the stuff of theory,
or dropped into oblivion —
an unpredictable
and unchartable passage
of time and matter
into the vastness.

NOSTALGIA

Antiques standing in a barn

Shadows, mist

Dropping fruit

Fires smoldering in a clearing

Drifting mind

Memory bent as

A stick in the water eluding

Grasp

Echoes reverberating

Ear cocking

Particles passing, waves sweeping

As easily through the mind

As through the galaxies.

CREATION

Were I to paint

the emptiness of the darkest night,

palette knife would have to laboriously

apply the paint to the canvas.

To bring light to star points here and there

and challenge the thick perfection of total darkness,

only a splattering snap of the brush would be needed

to send paint out in a random pattern of specks

over the impenetrable void.

9

Aubade

The Clothesline

Written to the Close of Day

Thanksgiving Morn

Revelation

AUBADE

Vita awakens
in the unfolding hands
of the rosy-fingered dawn,
eager to leap up and play
in the bright day glowing,
sure, that as evening draws on
she will be pleased
by what inspired her day —
wondrous things
seen and done
billowing
in words unending
as quiet presses
like the paws of kittens
and she drifts again
with purring peace
into the still surround
of pillowed sleep.

THE CLOTHESLINE

When the automatic clothes dryer broke down,
my thoughts went to the interiors of the simple cottages
that sheltered my forbears in early 20th Century Europe,
their drying laundry hanging close to the stove
in the dead of winter.
I think of them as I go outside
in a little warming spell at this winter's end
to put up the wash
on a clothesline
strung between the wooden posts
that support my cabin on a hillside
at the edge of a creek.
Muscle memory brings a tingle
to my wet hands as I lift
the clothes to hang on the line,
as when I was a little boy helping
my mother and my grandmother take out
and bring in the wash.

Hanging it out in winter
would sometimes dry it all stiff as boards,
but the weather is milder today,
as I press open the clasp of the clothespin
to connect the garments to the line.
I feel the heaviness of the clothes
pulling the line downward,

but almost immediately remember
the lightness they will have
after a day like this, so breezy and bright,
the air wafting the load and infusing within it
the fresh scent of the out-of-doors.

Indoors to outdoors,
across continents,
across time and seasons —
in my lifetime
and that of my people before —
here I am,
dealing with the wash in this old way again.
I pause to ponder it all briefly.
At the side of the cabin near the clothesline
is a tangle of laurels and evergreens.
And as the water laps loudly over the rocks in the creek,
it stirs up something more in me,
something in the chasm between touch and thought.
It is a sudden vision of the Fates
demanding my attention –
Clotho spinning the threads of life,
Lachesis measuring it out,
Atropos cutting it with her fearsome shears.
They are all here as I hang the clothes,
their bodies the shapes of the tree trunks,

clothed in laurel and evergreen garments,
all bent over and intent on their work,
moving with determined force in the breeze.

I feel my hands tingle again
as I go about finishing
the hanging of the wash.

WRITTEN TO THE CLOSE OF DAY

Amid the vibrant luster
of the last lit leaves of day,
I peer through the swaying
layers of shaded green
and gold, my old wooden pencil
to paper — paper once the stuff
of trees, now mottled sheets
in the shifting light
and shadows around me.
My pencil has become another
of the tree trunks
in the forest density, demanding
whatever is left of the light,
for soon the slowly enveloping
darkness will come to press
trees and pencil, leaves and paper
into lightless, wordless profundity.
And night will seal this day away.

THANKSGIVING MORN

I cannot throw away

what has been given to me

in the night —

an awareness that prods me

to get up from my bed

and set about expressing

what does not come with such urgency

in the ordinary light of day.

Startling,

it geysers from some dark, unknown depth,

hurling secrets in a powerful stream

high into the air,

the descending spray from which

may be a poem

in the dawn to come.

REVELATION

Slowly sliding through
the silent shallows
seemingly stalking —
                    a snake
lifting its head above the rocks.

Without turning to look,
it sees me and stops,
stone still.

My eyes sweep
over its form
as it unfolds its wings,
its brightening hue
going from grey to blue —
                    a heron
lifting itself high
above the laurels,
up over the shadows
and into the light.

ABOUT THE AUTHOR

Robert M. Giannetti was born in 1942 in Queens, New York and grew up on Long Island. He has been an Army officer, college teacher, garbage man, and business owner. Currently he resides in Lewiston, New York, where he owns and operates Bob's Olde Books. He is the author of a previous book of poems, *Drawn by the Creek*, published in 2003.

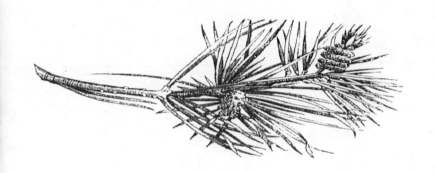